AF421371

QUIET AS IT'S KEPT

By
Na'Tosha De'Von

Cover Art
By
Shay Mac

Dedicated

To Emery:
20 years from now, may the confessions in this book
allow you to feel that you're not alone.

To Takkia:
Remember things kept quiet are things left unhealed.
Speak up when you're hurting, speak up when you're
happy.

The premise of my art is to expose and heal.
One cannot heal if you don't see the parts that are
broken. So, the exposure while brutal is a necessary
madness.

-Na'Tosha De'Von

Table of Contents

Quiet As it's Kept

I was eleven years old
when my pen and I became attached at the hip
The first time I allowed a metaphor to roam in my mouth was
to defend my depression
Even it needs a friend
Even it needs a partner
to balance disco balls and dance floors
I believe in God and my mother
Sometimes both seem too busy with the world
to communicate with me
I'm told they're there
I know they're there
So, I write things down
in hopes to read it to them later
On stages and airplanes,
both of which I'm terrified to touch
Afraid of the high
The more I give to words the more they reject me
They tangle in my mouth
like wide tooth combs in African hair
Naturally, we were supposed to work
Age 27 I will discover that I am dyslexic
What a relief
What a tragedy
Lacking in knowledge
Lacking in substance
Always lacking in something,
some things never change
I wrote this book on the high of a breakup
The low of revealing secrets to my family and I still have so
much that I kept,
so much that I've kept quiet.......

Let His Will Be Done

Mary never fully gave God permission to her body
I was told by nameless women in the Bible
that the day he cracked open her purity for his sacrifice
the first rose grew its thorns
After all, when a woman is deflowered in such a way
it makes sense that she'd grow spikes
in order to protect herself
They say her permission was given in a whisper
Leave it to a man to assume
he knows what's best for you
Glory be to the Father, Son, and Holy Spirit
but only grace was given to Mary
What a low blow
The short end of a blessing, the robe of misogyny
Of course God is male
Why else are we made to fall upon our knees
in order to please him?
There was a reason why the Jezebels in the Bible
were shown God's mercy
then later filled with His grace
Before this came Heaven and Earth
Isn't it just like a man to build something out of nothing
then dispose of it when it no longer serves his needs
And I'm trying to find the difference between God
and all of my past lovers
Because lately I've been told to have faith in their
existence although I don't see them much any more And
I have to wonder
if they're simply being led by the Spirit
If we're healed by the blood,
then how careless was it for God to allow that woman to
have an issue with hers
Maybe Jesus was trying to tell us something

when he sacrificed his
What if Eve ate the apple to rid herself from the garden
but could never quite free herself
from man's control?
Because there were women raped in the Bible
then later forced to marry their attackers
Women today are still forced in covenants
with their attackers
You see I think we've been getting it all wrong
What if masculinity isn't toxic, but rather biblical?
It's like the Word was too busy abusing the mother
So, for His forgiveness
God decided to bless the child
who managed to have their own
In this, Jesus wept, but no one else did
And I have to forgive myself on drunken nights
when I didn't quite say no
Forgive him for not quite hearing yes
Remind myself that woman will always be servant
And FAVOR is man
And I found savior,
I mean favor
In this moment just like Mary
I found favor, right?

Dearly Beloved

He made his way down
through the belly of the church
Fell to his knees and begged to be fed by her kiss
Even a touch would suffice as a form of mercy
to appease his hunger
She could only offer him loose scraps
from past lovers who died at that altar of her feet
Clutching the pear shape diamond
She vowed never to wear
Never to expose herself to mirror the others
who craved matrimony simply for name sake
She knew only of independence
Stolen from hidden gardens of the deities
used as a means to stay immortal
How could she choose love over power?
Beauty over emotional greed?
She tossed the bouquet into the fire
They watch the petals fall
as the roses burned to red dust
Neither of them spoke
He remained hungry and they both just knew.......

The Woman > The Religion

She reaches into the Earth and pulls out an ounce
of Mother Nature's forgiveness
Hidden underneath blankets
of bosoms, brown lips, and Muslim praying hands
Ran to the front of the altar
just in time to utter her last Catholic Hail Mary
The Christians whispered in disgust
for they were known
to judge sin prior to dancing demons,
brave enough to commit them.
Jehovah covered his eyes
Couldn't bear witness to fallen angels
seeking redemption amongst men
The Baptist praised this act; tears filled her eyes
knowing that she would always be guilty of Eve's sin.
So, she offered herself as sacrificial bait
to restore the standard
Only in this did the masses find peace
But women never found their place

Eve's Regret

Screw on the legs make the girl walk upright / cover the scars / hide the bruises /yes sir, no sir / teach her manners / to silence on command / that her voice is no voice anyone longs to hear / remind her that she is woman / that she be of sex, reproduction, and sin / by the Eve you'll remember her flaws / by the dusk she owes you life/ God made her second from borrowed parts of your flesh / The sacrifice / No gratitude / No grace / as a way of saying thank you she left you exposed in the nude / destroyed the heavens / remind her of this deed / that man is Alpha, superior / and this is how we've been structuring the image of woman since before Christ/ And I sometimes wonder if Eve regretted Adam more than she did the apple

Pro Choice

If someone asks me I will tell them that I am pro- choice / that I love my child enough not to let them embark on this tainted world / I will tell them that it hurt the day man made machines sucked the life out of me only to violently confess my sins down the drain / I will tell them a story of joy / and how for a brief moment I was able to protect you from the lies and blood stained promises gift wrapped by the Devil / I will tell them of your innocence / how you glowed like Choir Angels led by Lucifer / What type of Mother would I be if I let you take that fall / polluted upbringings contaminated by Earthly destruction / this world never deserved you/ but your death does not go unnoticed / the absence of your presence feels like broken virginities through gang rapes / I couldn't save my child, but I will find comfort in knowing I somehow managed to save its Soul

Stillbirth Breathing
(A Black Mother's Labor Pains)

She holds him on her chest flesh to flesh
he coos in her arms
They smile
She licks the tip of her finger
to smear away the red paint of afterbirth,
marking him prey
Then thinks to herself
My God,
I've birthed a target today.

In Another Life

When I hand the doctor over my body
It is cold and I am alone in the back of an alley
both legs dangling
out the passenger seat of the van door
Didn't have the proper tools
So he takes a spatula, an old hunting knife,
With a bottle of Jack Daniels
There is a switch blade on his left side
he assures me
he's only had to use in emergency situations
Like on the pre-teen girl
who carried her fathers drunkenness
between her thighs
With the tremble of his right hand
He whispers that in an effort to save her life
he lost them both
The infection caused by the hunting knife was too much for
her body to bear
I watch the assistant with a washcloth full of bleach
slide up and down the blade
He takes the blade pierces it through my cervix
Shoves an old gardening hole in my vagina
I cloth the bucket that sits near his feet
An unfamiliar pain surges through my body
Like punishment of allowing myself to get here
I leave my body like female rights in America
and watch the crime unfold
In another life I was raped
I got pregnant by a married man
who I fell madly in love with
only to find that I was simply a distraction
My cousin once touched me and never stopped
I was told that by bringing this child full term
that it would kill me
I wanted to keep the baby

but nothing about my life said I could afford it
I didn't want to pass down my mental disease.
There was a 50 percent chance
that the baby would be just like me.
And isn't it just like a mother
to prevent her child from suffering?
The father once told me he wouldn't be there.
I didn't want to struggle
like the single mothers I knew
The sand in the hourglass drained,
it wasn't the right time
I fear I would mother my child
the way my mother raised me
In order to break the curse I had to sever the cord
I was too young
I was too old
I just didn't want to have children
After the silence swallows the air
The doctor tells me of a brief time in history when
this procedure was performed in a hospital
How the nurse would replace the police scanner
with my hand
He picks the blood from underneath his fingernails
And in that moment,
I'm reminded that he's one of the good ones
I close my eyes and
I close my eyes and....
And....

Damn it, she's lost too much blood.

Family Heirlooms

Grandma Mary raised her eyebrow to say,
"That pie be for your grandfather, be best not to touch it"
My uncles whispered in fear of Black magic and Voodoo spells
used to keep Papa near
The women in my family baked pies and passed down the
ingredients to their daughters
and their daughters
I never learned my way around the kitchen or men
Baking pies always seem redundant
Love wasn't a curse I could conjure,
and I was way too proud to play pretend
Maybe that's why the men leave
I don't fry lust in my pork chops like Nana
My apron hasn't been worn
since a lover compared me to scrambled eggs
Said he wanted over easy,
Sunny side up
In rage I boiled
Burned down the entire house
with him and his complaints standing in it
Papa says all that rebellion will force me to be alone
I pick up the doll,
The one that reeks of his arrogance
Place the needle slightly in its spine
He screams.
I've come to learn I'm more like my Nana
than one would think
and there's more than one way
around a kitchen sink.

Forgiveness

I forgive you but my mother no longer likes you
She says your apologies are like
caution tapes at crime scenes
such a normality for the massacre you caused
She tells me not to trust you
That your ways are as barbaric as demons
defending God on the steps of Catholic Churches
You're due no mercy
Now save your soul
Swallow your truth like communion
In reality
You never wanted to be saved
Just a temple where you could be praised
and made holy

About The Missing

I've heard fairytales that women like me
Once roamed the Earth
with brown skin and rebellion
Couldn't keep them submissive
so they stole them by the dozen
"Where have all the Black girls gone"
My nana once asked
after preparing supper to an empty table
She calls to them as if their ghosts will return
before the food gets cold
We nibble on frozen chicken during the waiting time
In the silence I can hear their souls
searching for loose bodies
Rustling at the back door
Singing in the unfamiliar language of their abductors
I've dug through the hampers during my chores
Made sure not to mix the coloreds with the whites
The bleach tends to stain the fabric
Nana says in time we will mend it later.
"Where have all the Black girls gone"
She mumbles to herself
Peeking through the cracks in the kitchen blinds
We can hear them at the playground
The evidence of Double Dutch
Their voices echoing through the monkey bars
Mama says if you listen closely,
they're trying to tell us something
Something valuable about the missing

The Waiting Woman

I've become my burdens
We met on lonely nights that whispered
in white sheets and waiting
Time has a funny way of revealing passing moments
uncatchable to the eye
I've forgiven and blamed myself
The apologies sink through the cracks on the floor
Next to mud fallen from the bottom of boots
with grime and justification for unnecessary steps
I wonder if anyone notice
Would they dare to remember my presences
Will they step over my existence
I'm sometimes over my existence too
The cold slab of the floor reminds me of the unnatural chill
I once felt in my lover's arms
Just like with everything I stayed longer than I should
There's an emptiness in my throat
Unsure if its worth swallowing
Pills like that tend to get trapped in my esophagus
I've given too much to this moment
Too much to people who are willed to leave
Some took the furniture
Others took the paintings off the walls
My grandfather's old color TV
The one with the lousy static
and discounted dents on the side
There was an elder woman with blue tinted nails
who ripped the fan from the windows
The propellers still blowing in her hands
There was no blood
Ironically, the blade didn't snip her palm
I watch the others take the entire window pane,
leaving me supine
There's footsteps calling to me in the distance
Not sure if they're drawing near or if they're pulling away

Awaken...

The sun peeks in around 5 am
 reminding them of the night they spent together before
One hour left until his exit towards the luring unknown
that this world would create for him
Laying on his chest
She would trace the outline of his Greek brand
with her fingertips
Thinking that this must be the logo that
Black Superheroes wore underneath their garments.
If only she could provide a leisure of ecstasy
that would serve as a pillar of strength
 during his weakest moments
She stuffed parts of herself in his pockets
Made sure to warm his tea just right
So that even in his exit
there'd be an ounce of comfort
In those final moments he tossed and turned
Like ships unable to find their footing on water
Not unlike the false Gods
that surround him for distractions
She held onto him ensuring him of his safety
Reminding him that all he needed was home
The alarm goes off as the air escapes his lungs
He whispers in her ear
Just five more minutes
Just five more...

Dear White College Frat Boy,

You are no big man in hoodie, but I FEAR you/ when walking past you I cling onto my roots like handbags in shopping malls / clear the way for your SUPREMACY / all hail to monsters who wear Ralph Lauren, Lacrosse, and Privilege / walk in your father's shadow, silver spoon / daddy freezes bank accounts Elsa takes the blow / they will tell you that no woman was OBJECTIFIED during your house parties / that mommy wanted to be QUIET during dinner tables and discussions / call it fiction / blame not yourself / the bitch hair shouldn't have been so long if she had no means for you to climb it / didn't SOCIETY teach you that not all little girls want to be kiss a fucking frog / Pocahontas, Cinderella, Sleeping Beauty, I am a female VICTIM and you are now watching Disney / pay for her silence / like father, like son /Incredible, in some cases it takes over 14 years but there will always be a sequel to lessons unlearned / ATTACK her motives / alone in a room with 7 men, I mean who can blame the boy / The shape shift of sacrifice / one kiss no longer princess she now stands as a frog / Your aura brings no protection in fear I disguise myself as man / go to war with your views to bring dishonor to my family's name / You turn bear claw away at my bravery / When you enter a room I sink through chairs to dissolve into floors/ Never mind my presence, step where you please / you stuff children into convenient boxes, over stuff ballot boxes and AMERICA turns blind / sing your ballots / OH SAY HOW CAN THEY NOT SEE / today you bumped my shoulder / I understood your mother more as I sat quietly and dared not to make a peep /yesterday your father crumbled the WORLD with his bare fist / They all sat QUIETLY held your mother's hand out of reflex and dared not to make a peep.

Hometown Glory

.... I left and no one noticed
When I returned, no one welcomed me home

Accident Ahead (Rerouting Now)

Don't return the same way you leave,
Auntie Poodie said
the men will be waiting
If they learn your route
Learn your waist
Take that switch out of your step
Move like you've got places to be
In this you will appear too distracted for cat calls
Too preoccupied for attacks
No one dares to rape a woman
who's got places to be in the morning

Tangled

During the rape
She won't focus on the stretching
Her insides shape shifting like
the counterparts of Decepticons
She will numb herself from his hands
like a noose around her throat
She won't feel, but remember him
Instead it will be his voice
The broken in his eyes begging for her approval
Tell me you like it
He will pull out
Stand over her body
like the home project he's been trying to finish
but mommy was too busy to see
So, he grabs the duct tape
Hangs her remains like a limp noodle on the refrigerator
for the entire world to see
She's become his masterpiece
He will drag her to the van, go out of his way
 to isolate her smile
She then cuts off her ear
Offers it to the Heavens
to silence the sounds of his moans
But God, just like society wants nothing of her sorrow
It won't be the rejection but his smell
How his nectar sends out trigger warnings
to fight, flight, or freeze none in favor of her sanity
so she simply fades away
No need to live in the now
when the memory will meta morph into monsters
The monsters grow into the night the night becomes the bed
The bed becomes the sheets that she once laid on
and now she's forever tangled

How The Wolf Protected The Moon

She....
Sits wrapped in the arms of darkness
surrounded by space, time
No one dares to draw near her
too much midnight, not enough magic
Cold and alone but they demand her light
Men document their footprints
as they tread across her backside
They prefer women made of sunshine and day

He......
Man's best friend turned rage
unpacked and unassisted
comes from the wilderness seeking sanctuary
He stumbles upon her light,
the whitest shade of blue
pressed his fur against her silk craters
listened to her midnight round and full
Her luminous nature admired his howl
He becomes her protection
She sinks halfway into herself and smiles

Simple Saturdays

I've hemmed my satin skirt
The black one with the slit up the back
I stained my cheeks in rose petals and temperance
Stood over a gas lit stove,
a common fan blowing through the window
You said you'd arrive on Saturday
I prepare for you and Saturday
I shaved my legs
Pulled out the lotion you brought back
from the Farmer's Market
The one that smells of mercy and honeysuckle
I set a table for two
Denied my flesh
The urge to touch
To feel
You taught me to abstain until Saturday
So, I wait for you and Saturday

Date Nights In Detroit

I waited for you at the edge of midnight
Slipped my nectar beneath your nose
like party favors from the '60s
You were suppose to crave me
Be it of muse or addictions desire
With tongues too silk to confess
Say you love me
Feel me the way you do your
hands tucked deep within your pockets
Eyes groping my flesh
like it be the last piece of art on a dying man's list
You've wished for wishful thinking
Thought perhaps by chance
You could one day lay with me
And isn't it something biblical
in the way that only I can grant you this blessing,
And isn't it something spiritual,
in the way that only I can bring you to salvation...

Beyond The Flash

I was once your muse
The light behind the flash
Every click of your camera belonged to me
We slow danced in a gallery of insecurities
I wrapped in all my layers to be photographed
in the nude for you
There I was
In the palm of your heart
or maybe it was just your art
I never could quite tell where we stood
Do you still find me pretty?
I need to hear your lies over the filters
I give you my word
I'll believe them
I swear it to be true
I can still be a perfect picture if you let me
Pose just right for you
Angle my body as you please
You can still make a masterpiece of me I'll find my light
Make your job easier If you don't capture it
How is the world ever supposed to see me smile?
How can you look at the magic we create
and say that it is not worth
The take, the picture, the flash
Images used as past proofs of our existences
Proof that we touched
Proof that we loved
Proof that sometimes you need more than 1000 words
to fully say goodbye
Just promise me my love
you won't freeze our frame in the edits
That when you walk through an exhibit
you will stare at an empty space on the wall
Clutch your camera
and fill the frame with me

The Searching...

She stepped into her insecurities and wore them
like an old outfit hidden in the back of her closet
that never quite went out of style
Unsettling how the fabric still fits
They will label this moment as vintage
tell you that your soul is a thrift store
but only if you're willing to sell for cheap
Funny how upon arrival
everyone's method is to look different
but they all come out looking the same

City Blues

My city birthed Oprah
then chased her away out of precaution
couldn't stand anything that big and that Black
It's hard enough
to keep Negro women in check as it is
This city has streets filled with potholes
Mothers who instill the luxuries of welfare
onto their young like survival skills
My home is made up of Southern biscuits
and cotton fields,
the climate is always hot
The cops are often as crooked as the letters
The humps in our backs are from unpaid labor
We still chasing that "40 acres and a mule"
But it's home
It's the smell of Magnolia trees, dirt roads
Friday night football games
Home, where we all can't wait to leave
but somehow seem to stay

DEAR POET,

WAS HE WORTH THE ART YOU MADE OF HIM?

Take 5

Yesterday in acting class
we were taught the method of shrinking on stage
Impressed with my execution and ability to adapt
My professor asked me
how I connected to the material so well
I told her that Black women
had been shrinking themselves for years
Under the swift hand of Massa's whip
The piercing jealousy of the Missus
after he bared back to touch her
Shrink our insides for force fed children
Decreasing ourselves
within a Black man's insecurities
Silencing our voice for society's comfortability
Drop in the values
assess the problem
correct the flaws
Objectify our strengths to minimize the needs
Too dark to find our light
so we push ourselves upstage
and blend in with the walls
Block out moments for we know that they are rare
We don't run on Equity
life never gave us the points
But the role must be played
The story must be told
So, we take the scripts, follow direction,
and try not to cause a scene
One would say that our standing ovation
is long overdue

Dinner Theatre

Being Black is like going to an event
The address was missing on the invitation
You were told to bring a dish
but only if it's gluten free
The attire was written in hieroglyphics
you don't own the device to break the code
When you finally arrived
after being pulled over for no reason at all
No one eats your food
Instead, everyone stares at you for being late
and not dressed to their impossible theme

A Stigma

When a Black man is depressed / he will bury his agony
between the thighs of a woman / label her bitch, slut, his
mother / all the things that he despises/ friends will look
to him as hero / body count rise like water / call him
Harvey, destruction, forgiveness, anything but man /
familiarize himself with the dark side of the moon /
transforms the night / revenge falls upon extinction /
deception cons the bay into believing that nothing of
Earth exists / be alien, foreign / opposite and exactly
like his father/ masculinity floats, sinks, then drowns /
unaware how to swim to shore / unaware how to swim
to solution / roll up his problems in hope to blaze away
the truth / the community welcomes this behavior /
boys will just be boys and Black men will only be
/statistics / prison numbers / emotionally and physically
unavailable / no one will notice that his shadows are
demons / difficult to point out assassins in the dark / the
truth is he won't understand his rage / just that he feels
it all the time / the sadness / the isolation / the inability
to identify the body lying next to him / so he drinks /
because seeking help makes you weak / makes you less
of a man / substitute answers for grandmothers' prayers
/ the light inside of him ignites meta morphs into flames
/ engulfs the body / he now moves through life as ashes
and bones / A Phantom spirit of his former self / but you
call him Father, Husband, and even your Son / don't
you?

She Sings The Blues

My woman, my Black, my blues are broken
I've toiled with self-worth and belonging
I lied to myself thinking
I could be anything close to magic
What is a Black woman if not optional in regard?
What's in her skin
But sacrifice full of strength
and stretch marks from birthing
I've birthed galaxies
only to be thrown into the abyss
My tears have healed nations
but grant me no grievance
Suffer in silence
like your Nana taught you....
Black girl
I've been baptized and scrutinized by the ones I carry
The ones I've carried
carry hate for me
Can you feel the load of my burden
weighed down by society?
Hear the breaking in my voice
the confidence stifles by the second
It snaps like twigs in the dead of a forgotten forest
So, watch your step
Black girl
Tell me I'm good enough
then stitch up my scars over morning coffee
only to release me back into the day
I've prayed over my daughter's womb
hoping that when she gives birth
the world will lay her daughter
on the bed of protection they never quite gave me
They didn't think to give her

I've been too busy protesting to protect myself
I hand my reflection apologies
because just like the world
I sometimes neglect me too
What a shame
Trying to be human and a God wrapped in one
So, I close my mouth in hopes that
I won't say too much
Shrink myself in hopes that I won't be too much
Yet remember to carry myself self-enough
to still not be enough for you
After all
the world needs someone to blame
And while I didn't sign up
I chaperone this dance, they repeat the song
And the vinyl spins on and on and on and...

When Driving And Called The N-Word For Having The Right
Of Way

Inhale
Cry
Yell at yourself for crying
Walk into rehearsals
Wipe your eyes
Teach a diverse group of children theatre
They are changing the world
They will change the world
Go home
Pour yourself a glass of Yellowstone whiskey
Curse
Check your bank account
Spend over $100 (that you don't have) on new clothes for a
serotonin boost
Eat a donut
Feel bad about spending thus said $100
Meditate
Reflect on your ancestors
Drink more whiskey
Go back add earrings to your cart
Start a poem
Never finish the poem
Touch your body
You're ok
Exhale
He was just a racist
And this was just another day in Bentonville Arkansas......

A Generation's Love Letter

We've been told stories of your greatness
How you marched
on enemy battlefields with **Emily Dickinson**
signed by ball point pens
with literary bravery seeping out of your pores
They say, you slayed dragons
bigger than **Mark Twain**
breathed fire down the throat of **Maya Angelou**
gave her permission to speak
Strategically placed stanzas
at the feet of **Nikki Givonai**
But somewhere along the way
you forgot your worth got lost like **John Keats**
became a rolling stone
Left your only child in the hands of teenage mothers
never quite experienced enough
to bring them up properly
So my generation, we were never raised
We just kinda grew up
Don't bite the hand that feeds you
But your palm was often empty
You left us here to starve
Didn't take time to teach us how to fish
See they will leave you out in the cold
then become upset
when you learn how to warm yourself
I will not apologize for learning how to survive
We are but mere students
A product of our teachers
So how dare you look this chaotic perfection in the face
and say that it is not good enough
When we have always been good enough
Question, were you too ashamed
to visit the orphanage that you once built?

They say you slow danced
in blizzard storms with **Robert Frost**
Kissed the cheeks of **Margaret Walker**
Ran fearlessly towards
theories with **Laurence Dunbar**
Did you trip over words?
Take flight on Malaysian airlines
Cause you never got your postcards or your black box
messages to show that you even care
But we are told to look up to you
To value your absent presence
But did you for one second stop to think that one day
We would come to the realization
that a diamond really has no value
It's just a colorless stone
How disingenuous of you
to point the index finger of blame
My generation, we are not angry
We're simply misunderstood
They say that a child without touch turns cold
You must forgive us.

A Whole New World

My mother being made of African descent
who believes only in the fixings of Jesus
Once questioned if I had a therapist
I told her I have a superhero
Whose primary mission is combating generational curses
You won't find them swinging from the text of Marvel or DC
You will find them standing firm by my side
when the building is collapsing
And my buildings are often times like London Bridges
they always seem to fall
She then asked me if my therapist is a woman
I tell her my therapist is a shapeshifter
who transforms into dragon slaying
beast fighter of the night
When my depression grows fangs
My therapist is the wrecking ball
that leaves the monsters toothless
It tucks tail and cowers at their feet
She now wants to know if they're Black
I can only describe their color
as magic, translucent, flashlight even
On days that forget the morning my therapist reminds me
of patience and stability in darkness
My mother then asks if people like that exist
for people like her ......
I tell her that people like that
were made from people like her father
Who looked like her mother
that healed people like us which made them invincible
She holds her breath,
nods her head like one day she'll give them a try

SBIW

I no longer desire to be a
Strong Black Independent Woman
It's much too heavy of a burden to bear
I saw how it destroyed my Nana
and almost killed all of her daughters
Maybe I'm a bit too passive
But death by suicide
has never been that attractive to me

The Mourning After

Today I woke up and didn't want to be Black
It felt like media coverage
Its origin smelt like hanging corpses
from burning trees, roots still stuck in pavements
Much too heavy of a load to carry,
even with God's assistance
I found myself stumbling through shadows
much too dark to be pretty.
Them shadows be my own reflection.
I've walked on broken mirrors
Embrace the pain,
ignore the blood, and they ignore it too.
Mama says it's better to be considerate
than to label yourself a victim
so, I don't bleed on their carpets.
When asked how I trained my arteries
to clog themselves
I tell them that I don't
My oppression has always managed to be humble
and scream in quiet places
Some call it technique
Others call it strategy
This curse, I mean this color
is crossed fingers behind Satan's back
after a pinky promise gone wrong.
Open wounds taste like hand me down burdens
too big to stand in so they swallow me whole.
Now we cough up water
just to choke on resistance

The Morning After

Today I woke up feeling extra Black
Big Black
Super Black Bee da Bee'd
Black Black with one K
because three just seems too fucking unnecessary
Black like my presence offends you
Like you can mimic but my culture just isn't in you
Black like...
Damn, didn't we place them shackles on tight?
How them Black folks able to stand up right?!
Black like
Ahhh haaaa WE GOT YOU
Black like
everything ain't fucking funny
Black like, yes, it is
Black like,
Business, trailblazers, and world shakers
Black like
We invented that
And that
And THAT
like creatives and cookout CEO
Drop it low
Black like....
Yes Queen
I see you serving lip and shoe
Black like
my King I pray for you
Black like
you keep your reparations
I'll take world domination
Blacknificent
Black like God
Like excellent

Like forgiveness
Black like night
Like Africa and my ancestors
Black like joy
Like bellies filled with laughter
and Big Mama collard greens
Black like,
You better eat that food else you ain't hungry
I'm village raised Black
Like community, togetherness dipped in culture
Black like my history
that critics acclaimed critical
So they race to erase my race
to fit their cognitive theory
Black like I ain't going nowhere
Defiant, strong
I'm as Black as they come
Like Marches, Protests, and
Whoopi Goldberg's gums
I am Hella Black
Like my mother
and her mother and her great, great, grandmother
Who I'm pretty sure was once GOD

After Dark

Alysia calls at three am, wakes me out of my sleep
Said she could feel his hands
smothering her in her dreams
As he yanked down her panties
she woke just in time before the penetration
Nights like these are normal to a survivor
Nights when your abuser crawls in the bed
to lay next to you
He becomes your Freddy Krueger
You, simply the girl trying to stay awake
to avoid the torture
Avoid the nectar of his burn
But the Sandman holds you hostage
to the flashback in your dreams
Swaddles you like newborn flesh
She calls my phone because she knows that I, too,
fight the demons of the night
I am reminded of the time
when fears took over my own flesh
Like a child, I wet the bed before waking
80 percent urine
20 percent tears
My therapist said that this is normal,
And I want to be there for her
the way Jessica was there for me,
and Rita was there for her
Our attackers were once twins
not similar in face but identical in motives
They grew to be triplets
And most girls grow to find that all monsters look the same
when they show their teeth at night
I hold my breath, remind her to breathe
Wish I didn't relate to such nightmares, but I do
We share the sisterhood of the ripped off pants
It didn't matter that we were wearing pants

I once wished my denim
would transform into DemiGods
to protect me
But they never did
Instead, they took a trip,
traveled to one in every three girls in the room
Alysia assures me that she's now safe
That the monsters are at bay
She can return to her usual state of slumber
Now with the click of the phone
I can feel his voice racing along the telephone wires
to get back to me
I can see his fingerprints smudged against the mirror
As if to say,
you can never look at your reflection without remembering
Who I am and what I did to you
I walked back to myself
I slept in my walk I walk in my sleep
I tried to close the door Alysia opened
but his boot gets caught in the hinge
His presence fills the room
Familiar like he been here before
Like he knows exactly what to do
He sits at the edge of the bed waiting to enter my
Dreams as if it was a substitute to my body
I look him deep in the eye knowing that only one of us will
make it out into the morning alive
He smiles back,
assuring me that even then
he will meet me in my daydreams

Go to sleep you little baby
You and me and the devil makes three
Don't need no
other loving baby

Silent Rage

He lays beside you
belly full sack empty
both compliments to your care
You look over to see him smiling in his sleep
The disrespect
The blind content
No longer reaches for you in his dreams
You're just a probe
Just an object to prick
whenever his masculinity needs stroking,
with every stroke you feel more and more hollow
He cums,
pats himself on the back
but only after the sick fuck calls out his own name
You question your worth compare it to his genitals
and you think to yourself
He has to feel it,
he has to feel the exit laced within your touch

The Side Effects

The track marks of his handprints
are now smeared across my face
Standing next to fractured mirrors with bruises
I am replaced
Replacement so complacent
We put lids on broken jars in hopes that no one
will notice that we are shattered
Fingerprints left on my body cuts and scrapes of DNA
Soaking in a tub of water
there's trickles of tainted blood
One way reality looking at me
I tried to salvage what once was
But I save nothing
Yet somehow in this I've managed to risk my life
We go blow for blow
Round for round
No end to meaningless fights
Now.......
You're choking me, I can't breathe
I said you're choking me, I can't breathe
The canvas of my eyes painted black and blue by
the stroke of your fist I can not see
Somebody, save me
Counting how many times he promises
that this is the last time
I sign my signature on the obituary
I hand it over to him and I stay
Now we are high off hate
because we're sick from love
And my body has gone numb
I'm feeling ill as I take this last pill
and if we don't kill each other
then the side effects will

No Lifeguard On Duty

I'm considerate when I drown,
I know flailed arms and failing
That water damaged lungs are no good for help and hellfire
I don't scream out to the masses
I've learned that my choking on chlorine
only distracts the other swimmers
from the necessities of Marco Polo and Deep-Sea diving
I've fooled my loved ones into thinking
that I can breathe underwater
That somehow I can speak to the tide
and it waves back at me
That when the ocean opens its mouth
Reveals its teeth
I'm not bitten by the sharp edges of the shore
I wait until the others are busy with cannon balls
and back strokes
Tie an anchor around my ankle
Hold my breath, force my remains to the bottom
I sing myself a lullaby
just before the boat is overtaken by water
And even if by way of uncontrollable waves
My corpse rises to the top
I've already convinced those around me
not to see me as dead
But to simply think I'm just floating

Stagnant

He loves me like he's waiting for someone else
to take my place
I hold him like I pray she'll never get here

Not sure which one of us is suffering
Not sure which one of us is pathetic

Being A Poet

Someone once asked me
What is it like to create poetry,
to share it with the world...

It's simple,
being a poet is like taking rusty kitchen knives
while biting down on metal wires
to perform open heart surgery on yourself
No morphine or comfort of a nurse's grip
Just blood and battle scars
sulking in your own pain
Prolonging the process of healing

Sharing these words
are like ripping the scab off your own wounds to show
the public that you too know what it feels like
to bleed for the mistakes of others
That you know sacrifice
That an entry wound hurts just as bad as an exit
But they will mourn love upon leaving
never mention the wreckage
held by the hello of a tsunami
The fear that it brings
The waiting for destruction
The waiting for creation
The news will cover the story
but leave you to pick up the pieces
and call it a natural disaster
Some will even call this art.

The Art Of Letting Go

I picked up my pen to write about you,
It was the first time in months..........

My page however, is still empty
Some would call this writer's block,
others would call it closure

Restless Night

I find myself praying for her at night
After all, I once told you
I would always pray for your happiness
This is me keeping my word

Facebook Status:

April 6, 2012
Time: 10:33 p.m.

People keep asking why I date White men....
Well to answer your question,
I date Black men too.
But I am more attracted to White men
They have all the equipment and twice the cash
What can I say?
I like what I like
White is right honey

Years pass, lessons learned, love, knowledge, and
appreciation for my people grow.
Self-shame evolves into acceptance
Acceptance pours out into love

The girl above was hurting
with wounds invisible to the eye
Forgive me Black Kings
I didn't find value in you
because I was never taught that value in me
My Apologies
My Truth

One Of These Things Is Not Like The Other

I tried to assimilate
Stretched my voice into high pitch
Carbon copies of likes and totally's
Tried to silence the Negro in my smile
But the Afro in my dialect always seem to show up
at keg parties uninvited to
Thought if
I just put a bit of relaxer over my vocal fry
I could blend in with the White girls
Turned off all the lights and my
Marco would match their Polo perfectly
I convinced myself in this I wasn't drowning
Tried to date outside my Blackness
But the White boys would gift wrap me in lab coats
parade me around as in an experience
I used this Thesis Method to get back
at the Black boys who only saw their mother in me
Black boys who thought loving a dark skin girl they
deemed pretty was an exception
I hung between experience and exception
Leaving empty shells of my skeleton
in the Drive Thru
Told myself that this was White
I mean right
So I pulled up to the window
ordered multiple combos of Whiteness
that would fit inside my lunchbox
No matter how uncomfortable or unseasoned
I was determined to be an American
In a way that screamed success
that detached you from your mother
that echoed you made it out of the slums
Thought if I wore their clothes enough
they would ignore my Black ankles
peeking just above my tattered blue gym socks
But the work got too dirty,
eventually I had to roll up my sleeve

The more of me they would see
the less they would embrace
In my solitude I had to learn suffering and solace
It wasn't my reflection that I hated
Just the handheld mirrors society dug out of the gutter
to say that brokenness is all a Black girl could ever be
After my exile into the abyss
I went walking along the shores
Caught a glimpse of my image floating
next to Tefnut's memory
I smiled up at Shu, the Goddess of the sky
Felt my ancestors swoop me in their arms for my protection
Heard their voice crack
like lashes on backs of the unfreed
As they whispered
My child, you have always been enough
In your Black skin
In your African rooted body
So, I took a step into the water,
was Baptized in Blackness
No hand behind my neck to hold me upright
But I floated anyway
The World made no sense
But finally, I belonged

His Deepest Fear

He was born to a Virgo mother
women of that caliber always had the tendency
of making him feel intimidated
yet unbelievably loved
The way her perfection sits on display
like pickables from trees in springtime
She smells of chaos with a hint of stability
The only type of woman that made him believe
in astrology, horoscopes
and all its outwardly predictions
She was of the universe
Not deniable like Pluto
But concrete like Saturn, the Sun
She loves like galaxies
and beats a heart of black holes
but he can only understand
the Earth's slow rotation
Footprints on the moon was merely a myth for him
In his fear, he would flee from any woman
who mirrored her orbit
Wrapped in planets that hung from the sky
yet yearn for their closeness
through distant space and time.

A Poem About Kamala Harris

Look mommy she looks just like me

Baggage...

I carry the sins of my parents heavy and unforgiven
laced in pipes, gas stoves, and purgatory events
My mother a housewife
unsure by choice or religion
Took the blows of my father's leadership
Grace was something she wore best at dinner tables
Taught me the value of silence amongst men
While my father in his absence
exposed me to the world of imagination
Picture your mother sober
 what she would look like
without that pipe in her hand over gas stoves
Like daddy loved her more than his addiction
like the only way to grasp his attention
was to become a part of his addiction
Like we would have been enough for their souls
to seek sobriety before this life as children,
became all that we knew
So, I carry their sins
In the bottom ring of a shot glass
In blunts that my lips never became acquainted with
Through sacrifice and security of a designated driver
For nights when I see more of my parents within my friends
than I would like to admit
In my silence, I accept their behavior
The cycle switches gears but often never breaks

Human

I didn't watch them fall from the Heavens
but I deemed one more worthy of Earth than the other
My Father, wings broken
I gave no assist, no aid
Just judged his inability to fly
His lack of Halo
He had to be the reason she roamed the Earth
leaking feathers and sin
Didn't see that mother's detachment
from good and God
was based upon her own accord
They were both HUMAN
I, sometimes casualty
Sometimes love of their life
I've spent a lifetime creating lifelines of life lessons
And in this life, I've learned
Evil doesn't always come in shades of black
Sometimes it's baked cookies, forehead kisses,
and mentioning of sacrifice
Good isn't always pretty
It's staying away so I don't hurt you
Missed phone calls
because I just don't know what to say
It is doing your best in spite of
They loved me in spite of
I love them both
in spite of

A Sink Full Of Memories

I watch the memory part of her brain
iron itself into expensive silk
She wills it into a timeless piece
A scarf
I place the fabric into her lap for keepsake
I've held my hands under running water
to catch all the memories
that my mother can no longer hold
Then gently lean her mouth
towards the base of the faucet
and I beg for her to drink

Open Letter

An Open Letter
To the newfound woman in his life...

Did he promise you the same world
that he still owes me?

The Birthing Place

She tugs at me in the dead of the night
Idle minds lurking down translucent alleys
She be Chi
Till the lights come on
Force fed bullets
But she wears the bruises well
I miss her hands on Sunday Mornings
drenched in Rosary Beads
She smells of Bleach and forgiveness
I wonder would she recognize me if I return
Exchange money from loose cigarettes
for bus fares to get back to her
Remnants dancing under streetlights
I find her riding on the trains alone
She taste of mild sauce and poverty
Sits south along the Pier
That last man to love her and leave her lost his soul
In Golddiggers, Runaways, and Flashing Lights
I fear if I returned less than perfect
she'll disown me too

To Common, thank you for the words
that you inspired...

The Dreamer -The Believer

Even under blue skies you're too busy sleeping, speak up
Become the voice of the meek and underprivileged
Without permission or request form unions
so, in this revolution lets stand
Legs by legs bound in shackles
We plant roses in woods
hiding underneath the bodies of our dead mothers
weighing down her caskets
becoming envious to Solomon
because we have been a slave to this
for counting more than 12 years
Just tell me
Have you ever seen a nightmare
transition its way into a dream
Call your local sandman
cause they sleeping on us
They close doors......
We break windows
There's no sleep in this jungle we dream

And I wish I could give you this feeling I wish I could
give you this feeling, uh-uh
On the corners, niggas robbin', killin', dying
Just to make a living, huh?

Modern Day Sports

He once asked in his ignorance:
What did I ever sacrifice for him?

I told him:
You were a kick boxer without a punching bag
I sacrificed myself for you to train.
I did this knowing that you would never
miss a day of practice
Brutal, somedays I felt like it was worth it
When I got use to the combination
you switched sports
So I served myself up, volleyball
You spiked away at my self esteem
I became net
only good enough for catching your failures
Not a means for you to score
You began to look at me as enemy
Something to aim over
Over the fields I sat in the pits
waiting for a turn to be used
When bases were loaded,
I was knocked into the outfield
You scored, hit a homerun
Quickly celebrated with your team,
The moment was priceless, wasn't it....

The Ugly Truth

You will stand face to face with his demons
Call out their bluff
Demand the little boy in him step out
for his protection
He will see you
naked and exposed a thousand times
but still begs you to bare your soul
Like gravity wasn't already
working against you in some way
He wants more,
more than you could ever offer
You choose yourself over sacrifice and leave

CTRL +ALT+DELETE

Put down that pen silly girl
No amount of poems will make that boy love you
Those pages won't comfort your soul
Stop baring your heart like that......

QUELY

Drive safe
Call when you get there.

Home

Aight, cool love you

September 17,2017

Happy G Day

Thank you Boo

September 23, 2017

Can you check my oil
when I come home.

You still don't know how?
Man you trippin.

Bruh that's why I got you.
Come on man.

Toddy, stand down.

Home.

June 20, 2019

Don't put your faith in people,
they are going to let you down.
Put your faith in yourself and God.

It just hurts.

Don't give them no power.

November 26, 2020

I want to give you my kidney.
We got too much to do
for you to be sick. I need you
on the red carpet as my bodyguard.

Man, Toddy don't say that
I can't take your Kidney.

Not up for debate.
I will finish this play
while you focus on getting better.
When we done
I will take off for the surgery.

We gone look at other
options man.

Either you let them do the surgery
or I will cut it out myself
and hand it to you.

I love you too Toddy

December 31, 2020
Quely......

January 6, 2021

Coming home to see you
and say Goodbye.

I couldn't drive
without texting you.
I'm here Safe

January 8, 2021
I love you too Quely
I'll miss you forever.

June 14, 2021
Nothing's the same. We still need you.

When Grief Comes Home

It piles in the sink like leftover dishes
from catered parties three summers ago
You tell yourself you'll tend to it eventually
But the days bleed into the night
The blender sits unused in the corner
clogged with old bananas and flax seeds
So you hire a maid
But she's hours too late
You remove the dishes from the counter
Place them in the washer
Ignore their presence for weeks but the smell
The smell arises like rotting teeth
in an unkept wino's mouth
You keep it shut
Keep your thoughts to yourself
Spray Febreeze around the living room
Shift the focus from the laundry overtaking the walkway
The darkness overtakes and your legs become unable to walk
away from the decaying house
you've dressed up as a home
Call it farce when you lay on bed sheets stained by
the residue of latent lovers who've cum and gone
Men who step over hot Cheeto bags and empty water bottles
to escape out of the front door
Didn't think enough of your healing to simply put it in the trash
Leaving you with one less thing to deal with
A little less litter for luck
This mundane normality swoops you in like the candle
reflection from a television glow
as you binge watch the manic episode of current life status
New season, same plot
And due to all of this editing
Grief has labeled your body home

The Light, The Burn

I'm a candle
I'm a candle inside of a glass jar with no wax
So I'm just a wick
I'm a wick inside of a glass jar forever burning
So I'm just a flame
I see the wax I know it's there
but I smolder before I am able to pour into myself
You see I'm a giver
I sprinkle wax inside myself
but not as fast as the flame from the wick is ascending
People think that I'm lighting up a room
But overlook the fact that I am burning
I'm burning because I'm always on fire
I am a walking Hazard
There's a difference between light and a flame
Both can illuminate spaces
but one has to destroy in order to do so
In this body I burn to smut
No one seems to feel the projected heat
they're too overtaken by the glow
I am a hazard trapped inside of a glass jar
in a lit room with no smell
So I'm just flames and glass
But if you hold heat to a glass long enough
Eventually the jar will shatter
And there will be no light
No glow
Just charred fragments from what once was

7 Tips On Dating A Narcissist

He has a way of making you feel bad for mistakes he's made prior to knowing your name. You will discover this on your third anniversary two hours after he was supposed to show but didn't call. Blame it on your voicemail, the nerve of you to rush him. This reminds him of his mother, you are too impatient. Now suffer the consequences and spend your anniversary alone. `

Tip One: Don't cry. Too many emotions makes him uncomfortable. You are the love of his life and should never make him uncomfortable. Suck it up, apologize for being too overbearing, close your mouth, and take your dessert to go.

You will notice that he never yells. Only speaks to you in whispers, no one will believe what he burns in your ears. He loves you to death.
Never mention your bruises. They are from when he pushed you out of his life. Made it toward the edge of the door, yanked you back and said, I love you so bad you have to stay. Try to find ways to heal your rotator cuff without the means of surgery. When the doctors ask, how did your ligaments get so torn? He will stand there, scratch his head and reply, sometimes shit happens.

Tip Two: Doctors and hospitals only put people in your business, no one will believe you anyhow.

You're always writing about me, he says. The truth is toxic poetry is second nature to a poet. It spills out of the pen like jigsaw puzzles waiting for you to rearrange the words and letters. How can we make the pain of this relationship sound poetic to the ears, yet detrimental to the soul.

Tip Three: He mustn't know the trick of your pen, or he will beat the art out of you. Stain your aesthetic, convince you that you now have writer's block. The narcissist in him will then blame your page for not being Maya Angelou enough to craft through the pain.

Something about you has changed.
When you first met so full of light, speak nothing of torture. Your depression is depressing, and this only solidifies what he has been saying to you for years: No one can love you as much as he, not even yourself.

Tip Four: He invited parts of you, not all of you. Be considerate and pack lightly.

You see, the problem; when dancing with the devil, is he oftentimes has to be reminded that the music stopped years ago. So he will continue to dance until the soles of your shoes are worn out. The blisters on your feet will tell the tale of how you were just too tired, too beaten down to walk away. After all, he kept playing your favorite song. Or maybe it was the echo from the time before. He tells you that you've got no rhythm. But it is hard to keep up while bleeding through socks over kitchen floors. The cha-cha for you is too fast , but this man refuses the give and take within a slow dance, you drag to keep up.

Tip Five: Never wear heels. This only makes the task of date night difficult. Remember he will only always take you dancing.

The fights sound like conversations or maybe the conversations are sounding more like fights, I'm unsure as to which. Everything that spills out of his mouth seems to contradict himself. Even the way he says, I love you has venom and a price. You pay for his nature and insecurities. He will always be sorry for the things he's said after he's said them.

Tip Six: You will learn to carry forgiveness in the bottom of your purse. Pull it out on days like today when his tongue is more razor blade than truth.

You will look to the stars, astrology, and horoscopes for a sign. Somewhere, someone has to agree on this union, right?

Tip Seven: Don't pray to God for a sign, he has already given you six. It's clear that you will never walk away.

When The Narcissist Returns

When the narcissist returns
Grab a towel
Remove the boot print from the door he has
just kicked down to return back to you
There's something romantic
in how he lets nothing stand in the way
Not the door
The restraining order
Your voice begging on its knees for him not to
He will remove the spikes from his teeth
Place the thorns at the hem of roses
You will oh too willingly grab the bouquet
Ignore the prick
He will lick the blood from your hands
to remind you of what his intimacy feels like
You will slow dance with his demons
Remember the night they held your face
over an open fire
In an attempt to melt the tears away
Don't complain about the smoke
Instead, wipe the smut
from underneath your fingernails
Whisper to your sanity
It's ok, at least now you're no longer crying
He will kiss your battle scars for temporary acceptance
You will accept this as love
Reacquaint yourself with the mid-night
he has made of you
The dark
The lonesome
I mean how can he be considered a monster
when he's nursing your turmoil
He loves you
He loves less

You're worthy
You're worthless
You are worth less
to him than his ego
And at some point,
you can't keep answering his lonely
Breathe in his broken
So you cut off your ligaments
Limb from limb
Past the gristle through the bone
to prevent the urge of touch
But somehow, you're still connected to his demons
Like they got some kinda hold on you,
How you know their face
Call them by name
Then you realize
His demons were once your demons
Therefore they were born dragons
He only breathes fire because you lit the match
And through the rubble of torn cities
he has captured you in
He will hold a mirror of ruptured glass
to your face and whisper
How does it feel to finally love a version of yourself
When the narcissist returns
You will stand up,
walk back into yourself, and breathe

Only For Now

And eventually we will return to the celebration
The applause of togetherness
The warm sounds our hand created
when touching the spine of loved ones
One day we will tell our children about the year
the world went missing of laughter and confetti
We will teach them of birthdays spent
on our living room sofas
Kisses through glass windows
And how hugs became much too great
of a sacrifice to endure
We will open their history books
and turn to the pages that we made come alive
How we marched in a panic through pandemics
all for justice's sake
We will pull out our old mask
The one we dared not to throw away
because we just had to have proof
They will shake their heads in disbelief as we explain
how pieces of fabric kept the world going
Then they will understand
why we sanitize their hands a little more
Hug them a little more than we should
They will no longer question their privilege
But look to us as the Heroes
who brought back joy and confetti
And wouldn't that make it worth it
Their future should be worth it

What Was Taken

I don't know my mother's native tongue
I've lost the heritage in mine
Been washed out with soap
Scrubbed away by injustice
I couldn't tell you the warmness of it touch
The fingerprint falling on yearning ears over the years
We've lost this connection to home
I wanted to speak to my roots but I was never taught how
I didn't understand it's language
Went searching for who I am but the answers fell short
Tried to trace the trail back that my ancestors once walked
but I trip over the not knowing
Motionless and not growing
I grew up surrounded by oppression
Plantations stood on every corner
competing with the liquor stores
The alley way priest says Amen, I mean
I carry loose cotton and spare change in my pockets
for the life of me I couldn't tell you why
We traded in tribal knowledge for tribal wear
Impersonating the lives we were
always meant to live but didn't
In my resilience I rose to radical love resting on an
unknown connection that I cannot explain
When passing down the name of settlers
who bought my ancestors
To the children that I birth today
I usher forgiveness into the universe for knowing
not who I am and not what I do
For not remembering the past that was stolen
Yet protecting the future that is to come
I don't know my mothers face
but I am sure that she is out there searching for me
And in my disruptive radical love
I'm sure I'm making her proud

When An Old Social Justice Poem Will Do

The topic will be on racism
You will repeat these words
the same as you did during the last protest
It will prove that time has moved forward
But the issues stood still with their hands up
A bullet in their back.
A knee on their throat
When an old social justice poem will do
You will pull it out from the back of your trauma
tucked deep within your memory
Fail to question why 10 years later
the stanzas still make sense
Why the metaphors feel relevant
These words should no longer matter but they do
Now more than ever,
when an old social justice poem will do
You will find it drowning
wade in the water
It will trouble the waters
 like ghosts haunting the middle passage
It will be a bloody Sunday in 1972
The Black holocaust in Arkansas
Known and unknown news
They will cover the days of worship
But only if you include the bombs, the Negro bodies
The charred bones of four dead Black girls
Erasing the fifth
cause no one talks about the living dead
When an old social justice poem will do
It will fall on deaf ears
like the cries of weary travelers
Making their way through the Underground Railroad

You will find it swinging low from Magnolia trees
Like the sweet chariots
galloping their way into the depths of Mississippi
carrying the savory souls of Freedom Riders
seasoned by a Jim Crow South
Them boys be finger licking good on the trigger
but even better with a noose
When an old social justice poem will do
 The crowd will rumble
Ferocious like the belly of a Tropic thunderstorm
It is the brick in an adolescent's hands
tearing through community glass windows
It will be the tear gas that clouds your lungs
 The police club hitting your back
The disperse of defeated fighters
Stepping over the body of the slain
It is the silence
It is the siren
The contentment until it's no longer enough
But when a poet puts down her words
She will birth these metaphors
and bring them to the fight instead

Arkansas Arts

Local creatives gather at a Multicultural art event
The LatinX poet performs
the crowd cheers, she sits down
The third-generation poet performs the crowd cheers,
she sits down
The LGBTQ poet performs
the crowd cheers, they sit down
The Black poet stands
An announcement is heard over the intercom
she is told they've run out of time
The school bell alarm chases the audience out of their seats
Sirens blare like they're hailing unseen tornados
Like they're trying to prevent a storm
Like the catastrophic hurricanes
her words are sure to develop
Won't be welcomed here
Because when you're Black
Even amongst the minorities you are still
THE MINORITY
When you're Black, some Brown and Rainbow hands
are less likely to save you
When you Black, even amongst creatives
your expression has a limit
Your stopwatch turns into Grandfather Clocks
You can only perform on the hour, every other hour
There is a glitch in the safe space
we've been trying to create
There is still racism within the arts
Divide amongst the diverse
The way White artist mold Black sculptures
as if someone else can tell my story better than me
The Black poet holds back
the river of tears in her eyes
Uses her Maybelline lash as paddle boats
to steer them from her face
But the stanzas in her throat grow arms and legs
Crawls to the edge of her mouth

taps at her teeth
Tugs at her tongue
Like this be a fight for her ancestors to finish
Like the Maya Angelou that burns in her pen
be more than willing
Like Nikki Giovanni breathing into her lungs
to give it a go
Like her army filled with greatness
Be more than ready
But instead of giving the command
She swallows it down with an all too familiar
submission that only a Black girl knows
Because in the end,
the poet never needed your fucking stage
For she was a walking metaphor dipped in braille
And all who chose to feel her magic would.

>>> Insert Title Here<<<

Most men only truly LOVE me after they break me /
something about fragments and particles reminds them of
SACRIFICE / When I'm SAD I wear my grandmother's old
sweatshirt it smells like hospital beds, lost memories, and
REGRET / I wonder do they chase her in the afterlife / the
things she forgot to remember. Did she choose death over not
knowing / did the heirlooms meant to pass down float away
with the years / or did we just not have ENOUGH memories
worth holding on to / the day I burst into flames to PROTECT
my loved ones / I ENGULFED everything around me /
Eventually they COMPLAINED about the heat / how my
existence makes them perspire / why can't she just flicker and
not BURN like normal people / I FAIL at things I had every
intention at exceeding in / I turn people into ART then make
them stand in line to see / The nerve of me / I'm drawn to my
lovers' DEMONS they remind me of myself / the parts that I
keep BURIED / I overcompensate with kindness / the last
time I kissed a MAN it felt like
rubbing open WOUNDS across sandpaper and pouring salt
within the remnants / I was told to label this as LOVE / so I
took a rustic needle, few strands of thread, sewed my mouth
together, and SCREAMED to the top of my lungs / somehow it
didn't work / NO ONE heard me so no one knew / one
Thursday night I stayed up until 3 am writing love notes
DEDICATED to my MUSE and sticking them into a jar / most
of them were TRUE / others were how I wished he felt about
me / I realize that this isn't the line of a poem but simply a sad
FACT / most memorable moments in my LIFE are sad facts /
I dressed them up in METAPHORS and punchlines so they
will have a better MEANING / I ramble in my POETRY
because I'm trying to prove a point / somewhere between
reading and performing I'm sure they'll NOTICE...............

Enough

I'm attracted to broken people
If there is one thing that life has taught me is
This method of self-destruction
is because I'm broken too
Much of my self-esteem is rooted in the phrase
You look good for a darkskin girl
Which would explain why
I always search for the light
In people, conversations, and selfies
I'm trying to prove the compliments wrong
Trying to force that there is no truth in truth;
just perception
The last time a man told me he loved me and stayed
I was baptized at the altar
Call him Jesus
But this Messiah didn't swim
Couldn't float
Barely walk in purpose so he rejected the waters
Couldn't split from himself or the seas,
so he drowned
Didn't bother to take me with him
The rejection felt familiar,
it reminded me of my father
I fight to break this connection desire
more than my mother
I'm convinced that Black girls glow in the dark
I also know that one candle in a somber room
is not enough to light my path
I put a noose around the neck
of everything I questioned
My answers hung from old plantation trees
next to my ancestors' spirits
I breathe in their presence
I realize that life isn't just happening to me

And if it is…. isn't it beautiful?
Aren't I blessed to suffer amongst the living
rather than regret amongst the dead?
Doesn't my anxiety remind me
that I am capable of breathing
Even if it's too fast or too slow?
My depression that I am capable of crawling
out of dark holes and tight spaces
And in this moment of loving myself
I write down words in hopes to save the lost,
Heal the broken, and please God
I'm sure that when I tell them to strangers
I'm passing
I look out into an audience of people
with their demons sitting patiently in their laps
waiting for them to exit
They remind me that one poem
is not enough to save the world
But damn it,
it's just enough to keep trying

Special Thanks

To my sisters Serria and La'Chary, you are the representation of fearless Black women who nurture the world. It is not enough to thank you, so I honor you in all I do.

To the University of Arkansas 2019 MFA Acting Class. Your friendships I have carried, your gifts inspired me to be a better artist, and your support is unmatched. Thank you for your truth.

Thank you to Sipp Culture of Mississippi for being sponsors to my vision. The work you do is invaluable.

To Outspoken Arts Collective of Thee Jackson State University, thank you for being the foundation for so much of my poetry and truth. You taught me to create without apologies or disclaimers. I am forever in your debt.

Dear Quely,

I have attempted this letter more times than I would like
to admit. I stopped some days out of grief, some nights
out of anger. Other times I began to cry so much that my
eyes could no longer see the screen. Part of me feels like
writing this letter is ending a chapter, ending your
memory. I am reminded of what many great writers
have said, if you put something down on paper then that
thing can never die. So today I will start with a sentence,
and I will keep writing until it's complete.
I would like to say I've been ok. Tell you that I've cried a
little but for the most part I have really good days. The
truth is I'm not. The truth is, no one is ok. I watch my
sister try to pick up the pieces without her husband and
best friend. I watch your children knowing that they will
now have to be without one of the most important
people in their lives. I know my grief in comparison
seems so small but the hole in me is far from minor.
They say when you love a person while they're here and
never let them forget it, the loss will be less brutal. By
loving in this way you should have no regrets. In a sense
that's true but what they don't tell you is that you will
regret the future. I regret all the plans that I am so
fearful of taking without you. I regret knowing that in
my days to come you won't be by my side. I think we
mourn the past and grieve the future. While presently
we just try to survive. I replay the last thing you said to
me "I love you too Toddy" over and over. That
conversation so full of love and lingering goodbyes
brings me comfort in knowing that there was nothing we
wouldn't do for each other.

There are so many things I want to say in this letter, the most important being thank you. I remember so clearly when you came into my life and unlike most men of importance you stayed. You have always been my biggest supporter, and the person I would go to when I needed a self-esteem boost in my career choice. I can vividly hear you saying "Serria when we get our house, we have to get a room for Toddy cause she is not gone let us be without her" we would all laugh, but the truth is I always felt like your additional child. I can honestly say since you've been gone, I have never felt so exposed and vulnerable in my life. There's a certain level of emptiness that I can't explain. I never knew until you, that no one really has the words to make it better. Thank you for loving me that much. I promise to honor you in all I do. In all my biggest moments in life I will keep your memory alive. When I'm not doing enough, I will search for your voice saying "You better give them people hell, that's the only way". When I am doing too much as we both know I can do, I will hear you say "Toddy, stand down". I love you and my life was made better by knowing you.

To my readers.....
Before you close this book please join me for a small self-ca
check. Take a deep breath, let's inhale and exhale. Give you
mind and body the space it needs to process. Depending on
where you are in life, some of the content in this book may
have been a lot to take in. I acknowledge and I see you.
Thank you for going on this journey with me. Thank you fo
being open to the concept of true self exposure and all of its
complex flaws. May you carry grace on your path as you
strive to the other side of healing. Know that your journey i
one of many and that you are never truly alone. I am
Na'Tosha De'Von and you have been phenomenal.

Na'Tosha De'Von was born in Chicago, Illinois with a rich upbringing in Kosciusko, Mississippi. The actor and poet holds an MFA in Acting from the University of Arkansas as well as a Bachelor's degree in Speech Communication and Theatre from Jackson State University. Na'Tosha got her start in poetry as a young girl using it as a method of healing and self-discovery. Na'Tosha currently resides in Northwest Arkansas and spends her spare time going to museums and listening to jazz music.